Dedication

To all those who ever struggled with learning a foreign language and to Wolfgang Karfunkel

Also by Yatir Nitzany

Conversational Spanish Quick and Easy

Conversational Italian Quick and Easy

Conversational French Quick and Easy

Conversational Portuguese Quick and Easy

Conversational German Quick and Easy

Conversational Polish Quick and Easy

Conversational Hebrew Quick and Easy

Conversational Yiddish Quick and Easy

Conversational Arabic Quick and Easy
Classical Arabic

Conversational Arabic Quick and Easy
Lebanese Dialect

Conversational Arabic Quick and Easy
Palestinian Dialect

Conversational Arabic Quick and Easy
Egyptian Dialect

Conversational Arabic Quick and Easy
Jordanian Dialect

Conversational Arabic Quick and Easy
Emirati Dialect

Conversational Arabic Quick and Easy
The Spoken Arabic of Israel

Conversational Armenian Quick and Easy

THE MOST INNOVATIVE AND REVOLUTIONARY TECHNIQUE TO MASTER CONVERSATIONAL ARMENIAN

YATIR NITZANY

Copyright © 2017
Yatir Nitzany
All rights reserved.
EAN-13: 978-1-951244-22-41

Printed in the United States of America

Foreword

About Myself

For many years I struggled to learn Spanish, and I still knew no more than about twenty words. Consequently, I was extremely frustrated. One day I stumbled upon this method as I was playing around with word combinations. Suddenly, I came to the realization that every language has a certain core group of words that are most commonly used and, simply by learning them, one could gain the ability to engage in quick and easy conversational Spanish.

I discovered which words those were, and I narrowed them down to three hundred and fifty that, once memorized, one could connect and create one's own sentences. The variations were and are *infinite*! By using this incredibly simple technique, I could converse at a proficient level and speak Spanish. Within a week, I astonished my Spanish-speaking friends with my newfound ability. The next semester I registered at my university for a Spanish language course, and I applied the same principles I had learned in that class (grammar, additional vocabulary, future and past tense, etc.) to those three hundred and fifty words I already had memorized, and immediately I felt as if I had grown wings and learned how to fly.

At the end of the semester, we took a class trip to San José, Costa Rica. I was like a fish in water, while the rest of my classmates were floundering and still struggling to converse. Throughout the following months, I again applied the same principle to other languages—French, Portuguese, Italian, and Arabic, all of which I now speak proficiently, thanks to this very simple technique.

This method is by far the fastest way to master quick and easy conversational language skills. There is no other technique that compares to my concept. It is effective, it worked for me, and it will work for you. Be consistent with my program, and you too will succeed the way I and many, many others have.

Contents

Introduction to the Program 8

Introduction to the Armenian Language 11

Memorization Made Easy 12

Pronunciation of the Armenian Language 13

Note to the Reader 14

The Program 16

Building Bridges 38

Now you are on your own 43

Conclusion 45

INTRODUCTION TO THE PROGRAM

People often dream about learning a foreign language, but usually they never do it. Some feel that they just won't be able to do it while others believe that they don't have the time. Whatever your reason is, it's time to set that aside. With my new method, you will have enough time, and you will not fail. You will actually learn how to speak the fundamentals of the language—fluently in as little as a few days. Of course, you won't speak perfect **Armenian** at first, but you will certainly gain significant proficiency. For example, if you travel to **Armenia**, you will almost effortlessly be able engage in basic conversational communication with the locals in the present tense and you will no longer be intimidated by culture shock. It's time to relax. Learning a language is a valuable skill that connects people of multiple cultures around the world —and you now have the tools to join them.

How does my method work? I have taken twenty-seven of the most commonly used languages in the world and distilled from them the three hundred and fifty most frequently used words in any language. This process took three years of observation and research, and during that time, I determined which words I felt were most important for this method of basic conversational communication. In that time, I chose these words in such a way that they were structurally interrelated and that, when combined, form sentences. Thus, once you succeed in memorizing these words, you will be able to combine these words and form your own sentences. The words are spread over twenty pages. In fact, there are just nine basic words that will effectively build bridges, enabling you to

Introduction to the Program

speak in an understandable manner (please see Building Bridges). The words will also combine easily in sentences, for example, enabling you to ask simple questions, make basic statements, and obtain a rudimentary understanding of others' communications. I have also created Memorization-Made-Easy Techniques for this program in order to help with the memorization of the vocabulary. Please see Reading and Pronunciation in order to gain proficiency in the reading and pronunciation of the Armenian language prior to starting this program.

My book is mainly intended for basic present tense vocal communication, meaning anyone can easily use it to "get by" linguistically while visiting a foreign country without learning the entire language. With practice, you will be 100 percent understandable to native speakers, which is your aim. One disclaimer: this is not a grammar book, though it does address minute and essential grammar rules (please keep your eyes peeled for grammar footnotes at the bottom of each and every page of the program). Therefore, understanding complex sentences with obscure words in Armenian is beyond the scope of this book.

People who have tried this method have been successful, and by the time you finish this book, you will understand and be understood in basic conversational Armenian. This is the best basis to learn not only the Armenian language but any language. This is an entirely revolutionary, no-fail concept, and your ability to combine the pieces of the "language puzzle" together will come with great ease, especially if you use this program prior to beginning a Armenian class.

This is the best program that was ever designed to teach the reader how to become conversational. Other conversational programs will only teach you phrases. But this is the only program that will teach you how to create your own sentences for the purpose of becoming conversational.

THE ARMENIAN LANGUAGE

The Armenian language is an Indo-European language spoken by the Armenians. It has its own unique script, the Armenian alphabet, introduced in 405 AD by Mesrop Mashtots.

Like Hellenic Greek, it has its own unique branch in the language tree. It is the official language of Armenia and the Nagorno-Karabakh Republic. It has historically been spoken throughout the Armenian Highlands and today is widely spoken in the Armenian diaspora. There are estimated to be eight to twelve million speakers worldwide while the sovereign Republic of Armenia has a population of around three million people.

The country is based in the South Caucasus region of Eurasia. Located in West Asia in the Armenian Highlands, it is bordered by Turkey, Georgia, the de facto independent Nagorno-Karabakh Republic, Azerbaijan, Iran, and Azerbaijan's exclave of Nakhchivan. The Republic of Armenia constitutes only one-tenth of historical Armenia.

Armenia was a monolingual country by the second century BC. Its language has a long literary history, with a fifth-century Bible translation as its oldest surviving text. Its vocabulary has been influenced by Western Middle Iranian languages, particularly Parthian, and to a lesser extent by Greek, Persian, and Arabic throughout its history. There are two standardized modern literary forms, Eastern Armenian and Western Armenian, with which most contemporary dialects are mutually intelligible.

Spoken in: Armenia

MEMORIZATION MADE EASY

There is no doubt the three hundred and fifty words in my program are the required essentials in order to engage in quick and easy basic conversation in any foreign language. However, some people may experience difficulty in the memorization. For this reason, I created Memorization Made Easy. This memorization technique will make this program so simple and fun that it's unbelievable! I have spread the words over the following twenty pages. Each page contains a vocabulary table of ten to fifteen words. Below every vocabulary box, sentences are composed from the words on the page that you have just studied. This aids greatly in memorization. Once you succeed in memorizing the first page, then proceed to the second page. Upon completion of the second page, go back to the first and review. Then proceed to the third page. After memorizing the third, go back to the first and second and repeat. And so on. As you continue, begin to combine words and create your own sentences in your head. Every time you proceed to the following page, you will notice words from the previous pages will be present in those simple sentences as well, because repetition is one of the most crucial aspects in learning any foreign language. Upon completion of your twenty pages, congratulations, you have absorbed the required words and gained a basic, quick-and-easy proficiency and you should now be able to create your own sentences and say anything you wish in Armenian. This is a crash course in conversational Armenian, and it works!

ARMENIAN PRONUNCIATION

* In Armenian, there are thirty-nine letters and they all correspond to different sounds. In transliteration, therefore, various diphthongs are used to substitute those letters. Here is a list of transliteration rules that I used, and the description of how they should be pronounced.

A - [a] (aunt)
B - [b] (boy)
G - [g] (gig)
D - [d] (do)
Ye - [ye] (yet)
Z - [z] (rose)
E - [e] (every)
y - [ə] (about)
T - [t] (talk)
Zh - [ʒ] (vision)
I - [I] (see)
L - [l] (light)
Kh - [x] (like in Hebrew)
Ts - [ts]
K - [k] (like in Spanish como)
H - [h] (how)
Dz - [dz] (like Italian zia, zanzara)
Gh - [ʁ] (like french rouge)
Ch - (like ch but without aspiration)
M - [m] man
Y - [y] (canyon, you)
N - [n] (new)
Sh - [ʃ] (ship)
Ch - [ch] (cherry)
P - [p] (like Spanish poco, padre)
J - [dʒ] (judge)
R - [r] (like Spanish roso)
S - [s] (son)
*V - [v] (velvet)
T - [t] (like Spanish todo or Italian tutti)
r - [ɾ] (like Spanish arena, pero)
Ts - [ts] (like modern British tell)
U - [u] (room)
P - [p] (pen, poor)
Q - [k] (king, quality)
O - [o] (all, over)
F - [f] (father)

Again, this is not a pronunciation book. The sole purpose of this book is to provide you with the necessary skills in order to engage in fluent conversational communications. With regards to grammar and pronunciation, you are on your own!

13

NOTE TO THE READER

The purpose of this book is merely to enable you to communicate in Armenian. In the program itself (pages 16-40) you may notice that the composition of some of those sentences might sound rather clumsy. This is intentional. These sentences were formulated in a specific way to serve two purposes: to facilitate the easy memorization of the vocabulary and to teach you how to combine the words in order to form your own sentences for quick and easy communication, rather than making complete literal sense in the English language. So keep in mind that this is not a phrase book!

As the title suggests, the sole purpose of this program is for conversational use only. It is based on the mirror translation technique. These sentences, as well as the translations are not incorrect, just a little clumsy. Latin languages, Semitic languages, and Anglo-Germanic languages, as well as a few others, are compatible with the mirror translation technique.

Many users say that this method surpasses any other known language learning technique that is currently out there on the market. Just stick with the program and you will achieve wonders!

Note to the Reader

Again, I wish to stress this program is by no means, shape, or form a phrase book! The sole purpose of this book is to give you a fundamental platform to enable you to connect certain words to become conversational. Please also read the "Introduction" and the "About Me" section prior to commencing the program.

In order to succeed with my method, please start on the very first page of the program and fully master one page at a time prior to proceeding to the next. Otherwise, you will overwhelm yourself and fail. Please do not skip pages, nor start from the middle of the book.

It is a myth that certain people are born with the talent to learn a language, and this book disproves that myth. With this method, anyone can learn a foreign language as long as he or she follows these explicit directions:

* Memorize the vocabulary on each page

* Follow that memorization by using a notecard to cover the words you have just memorized and test yourself.

* Then read the sentences following that are created from the vocabulary bank that you just mastered.

* Once fully memorized, give yourself the green light to proceed to the next page.

Again, if you proceed to the following page without mastering the previous, you are guaranteed to gain nothing from this book. If you follow the prescribed steps, you will realize just how effective and simplistic this method is.

THE PROGRAM

Let's Begin! "Vocabulary"
(memorize the vocabulary)

I | I am	Yes/ Yes em
With you	Qez het (qez – you, het - with)
With him / with her	Nra het (nra – her, het - with)
With us	Mez het (mez – us, het - with)
For you	Qez hamar / (Plural) Dzez hamar (hamar - for)
Without him	Arants nra
Without them	Arants nrants
Always	Misht
Was	Er
This, This is	Sa, Sa e, (Plural) Sranq, Sranq en
You	(informal) Du/ (formal, plural) Duq
Sometimes	Yerbemn / (informal) Mek-mek
Today	Aysor
Are you / you are	(informal)Du/Du es(formal, plural)Duq/Duq eq
Better	Aveli lav (aveli - more, lav - good)
These	Sranq
He / She	Na
From	(noun) - Its *(read footnote)*

Sentences from the vocabulary (now you can speak the sentences and connect the words)

I am with you
Yes qez het em /Yes dzez het em (plural) *(Yes - I, qez - you, het - with, em - am)*

This is for you
Sa qez hamar e *(Sa - this, qez - you, hamar - for, e - is)*

I am from Armenia
Yes Hayastanits em

Are you from Yerevan?
Du Yerevanits es?
Duq Yerevanits eq? (plural)

Sometimes you are with us at the mall
Yerbemn du mez het es molum

I am always with her
Yes misht nra het em *(Yes - I, misht - always, nra - her, het - with, em - am)*

Are you without them today?
Du arants nrants es aysor?
(Du - you, arants - without, nrants - them, es - are, today - aysor)

Sometimes I am with him
Yerbemn yes nra het em
(nra - him, het - with, em - am)

*In Armenian, the place and time adverbs must precede the rest of the sentence
*In Armenian, the auxiliary verb is placed at the end of the sentence, "I am with you" *Yes qez het em (Yes – "I," qez – "you," het – "with," em – "am")* and the pronoun and preposition are usually flipped:
-"with you" – *qez /*"you") *het /*"with", -"for you" – *qez /*"you") *hamar /*"for", -"with the boy" – *tghai /*"us") *het /*"with"

*"From" / *its* becomes a suffix to the noun; e.g. Madridits – from Madrid, Annaits – from Anna)

I was	Ei / Yes ei
To be	Linel
Here	Aystegh
Same	Nuyn
Good/ Okay	Lav
Day	Or
It's	Da
And	Yev / u
Between	Mijev
Now	Hima
Later / After	Heto / Aveli ush
If	Yete
Yes	Ayo / Ha
Then	Heto
Tomorrow	Vaghy
Very	Shat
Also/ too/ as well	El, nuynpes

If it's later, better tomorrow!
Yete ush e, aveli lav e vaghy!
This is also good
Sa el e lav
It is the same
Da nuynn e
Yes, you are very good
Ayo, du shat lavn es
I am here with them
Yes yeghel em aystegh nrants het
The same day
Nuyn ory [orə]

*The preposition will always be placed after the subject and preceding the noun. "Sometimes you are with us at the mall" / *Yerbemn du mez het es molum.* First the subject, and then all the remaining parts of speech.

* In Armenian, the accent is usually on the last syllable so you stress the last syllable. This means that the accentuation is on the last syllable. In Spanish, it is on the penultimate syllable.

*In Armenian, the article "the" doesn't exist. At the end of the noun, a letter pronounced as [ə] is added instead. In transliteration, this letter is substituted by Y. Note, not to be confused with the Y that is read as *You* or *Year*.

The Program

Maybe	Karogh e patahel / Migutse
I go	Yes gnam
Even if	Yete nuynisk
Afterwards	Heto
Worse	Aveli vat
Where	Vortegh / Ur (where to)
Everything	Ameninch
Somewhere	Inch vor tegh / Mi tegh
What	Inch
Almost	Hamarya
There	Ayntegh

Afterwards is worse
Heto aveli vat e
Even if I go now
Nuynisk yete yes gnam hima
Where is everything?
Vortegh e ameninch?
Maybe somewhere
Karogh e inch vor tegh /
Karogh e mi tegh
Where are you?
Vortegh es?
You and I
Du u yes
What is this?
Inch e sa?

House / home	Tun
In / at	Um / -in / mej
Car	Avtomeqena / meqena / avto
Already	Arden
Good morning	Bari luys
How are you?	Inchpes es?
Where are you from?	Vorteghits es?
Me	Yes / indz
Hello / hi	Barev / voghjuyn
What is your name?	Anund inch e?
How old are you?	Qani tarekan es?
Son	Vordi / tgha (boy)
Daughter	Dustr / aghjik (girl)
Your	Qo (Plural, formal) Dzer
But / however	Bayts
Hard	Kosht(hard object)/dzhvar(difficult)
Still	Der

She is without a car, maybe she is still at the house?
Na arants meqena e, migutse na der tann e?

I am already in the car with your son and daughter
Yes arden meqenayi mej em, dzer tghayi yev aghjka het

Hello, what is your name?
Barev, anund inch e (*anun - name, inch - what, e - is*)?

How old are you?
Qani tarekan es?

This is very hard
Sa shat dzhvar e

It's not impossible
Da anhnar che

Where are you from?
Vorteghits es?

*In Armenian, "in" / "at" are not always used as separate words. Often the endings -*um* / *-in* are added to nouns instead. For example, "in America" / *Amerikayum*, "street" / *poghots*, "at the street" / *poghotsum*, "table" / *seghan*, "at the table" / *seghanin*.

*In Armenian, the preposition precedes the noun. The sentence above, "I am already in the car with your son and daughter" / *Yes arden meqenayi mej em, dzer tghayi yev aghjka het*, since "in the car" translates as *meqenai mej*. In Armenian, you have to first put the place adverb, and then the preposition "in" / *me*. There is no other way to say "in the car" than that.

Thank you	Shnorhakalutyun / Mersi
For	Hamar
For (*a person*)	Hamar
That, that is	Da / Ayd / Ayn / Ayn e
Time	Zhamanak
Our	Mer
No	Voch / Che
I am not	Yes chem
Away	Heru
Late	Ush
Similar	Nman
Other / Another	Urish
Side	Koghm
Until	Minchev
Yesterday	Yerek
Without us	Arants mez
Since	(*time*)-its (e. g. since April - aprilits)
Not	Voch
Before	Minchev / Nakhqan

Thanks for anything
Shnorhakalutyun amen inchi hamar
I am not here, I am away
Yes ayntegh chem, yes heru em
That is a similar house
Da nman tun e
I am from the other side
Yes myus koghmits em
I was here last night
Yes aystegh ei antsats gisher

I say / I am saying	Yes asum em
What time is it?	Zhamy [ʒamə] qanisn e?
I want	Yes uzum em
Without you	Arants qez
Everywhere	Amen tegh / amenureq
I go / I am going	Yes gnum em
With	Het
My	Im
Cousin	(Read footnote)
I need	Indz petq e / kariq unem
Right now	Hima / Anmijapes
Night / evening	Gisher / yereko
To see	Tesnel
Light	Luys
Outside	Drsum
I must	Yes petq e / yes partavor em / yes stipvats em
During	Yntatsqum
I see / I am seeing	Yes tesnum em
Happy	Yerjanik / Bari *(see footnote)*
There	Ayntegh

I am saying no / I say no
Yes asum em voch / Asum em voch
I want to see this in the day
Yes uzum em tesnel sa tsereky [tseréka]
I see this everywhere
Yes tesnum em sa amenureq / amen tegh
I am happy without my cousins here
Yes yerjanik em arants im yeghbayrneri/quyreri aystegh
I need to be there at night
Yes petq e linem ayntegh gishery [giʃérə]
I see light outside house
Yes tesnum em luys tanits durs
(luys - light, tanits - from house, durs - outside)
What time is it right now?
Qanisn e zhamy [ʒámə] hents hima?
(qanisn - how much, e - is, zhamy - the hour)

* In Armenian, there is no general word for cousin. You have to specify exactly how the person is related to you. In general, though, you can simply say brother/sister.

*In Armenian, the auxiliary verb is placed at the end of the sentence, however, in the event a second verb is present, it will supersede this rule and the verb will precede that second verb. "I want to see this in the day" / *Yes uzum **em** tesnel sa tsereky.*

*Bari is used to signify "good," such as *Bari Nor Tari* - "Happy New Year."

* This isn't a phrase book! The purpose of this book is solely to provide you with the tools to create your own sentences!

Place	Tegh
Easy	Hesht
To find	Gtnel
To look for / to search	Pntrel / man gal
Near / Close	Mot
To wait	Spasel
To sell	Vacharel
To use	Ogtagortsel
To know	Imanal
To decide	Voroshel
Between	Mijev
Two	Yerku
To	(read footnote)
That (*conjunction*)	Vor

This place is easy to find
Ays teghy [téʁə] hesht e gtnel
I want to wait until tomorrow
Yes uzum em spasel minchev vaghy [váʁə]
It's easy to sell this table
Hesht e vacharel ays seghany [seʁánə]
I want to use this
Yes uzum em ogtagortsel sa
I want know where is this house
Yes uzum em imanal, vortegh e ays tuny
I need to know that everything is ok
Indz petq e imanal, vor ameninch lav e

*In the last sentence, "that" is used as a conjunction, *vor*.
"**To**" - *Mot* ("come **to** me" - *ari indz mot*) / *Hamar* ("aimed **to** improve" - *lavatsnelu hamar*) / *Vor* ("**to** be able" - *vor karoghanal*)
*In Armenian, the "am," "are," "is" auxiliary verbs proceed the verb. In this case, instead of the verb we have "(it) is easy," which in Armenian will be *hesht* ("easy") *e* ("it is"). So *e* goes after *hesht*, as in the case with verbs.

Because	Vorovhetev/(informal) vortev
To buy	Gnel
Both	Yerkusn el
Them / They / Their	Nrants / nrantq / nrants
Each / Every	Amen
Book	Girq
Mine	Im
To understand	Haskanal
Problem / Problems	Problem / problemner
I do / I am doing	Yes anum em
Of	It's, i (read footnote)
To look	Nayel
Myself	Yes / inqs
Like this	Ayspes
Food	Uteliq
Water	Jur [dʒ ur]
Hotel	Hyuranots
I like	Indz dur e galis / yes sirum em

I like this hotel
Indz dur e galis ays hyuranotsy
I want to look at the beach
Yes uzum em nayel loghapin
I want to buy a bottle of water
Yes uzum em gnel mi shish jur
I do it like this each day
Yes anum em ayspes amen or
That is the book, and that book is mine
Da girq e, yev ayd girqn imn e
I need to understand the problem
Indz petq e haskanal problemy
From the hotel I have a view of the city
Hyuranotsits yes unem qaghaqi tesaran
I can work today
Yes karogh em ashkhatel aysor
I do my homework
Yes anum em im tnayin ashkhatanqy

*"Of" - (noun)-*its*, (e.g. "stone" - *qar*, made of stone - *qarits*) / (noun)-*i* ("piece of stone" - *qari ktor*)
*In Armenian to signify "problem" we use *problem / problemner*, however *khndir / kndirner* may be used as well.

There is / There are	Ka / Kan
Family	Yntaniq [əntanik]
Parents	Tsnoghner
Why	Inchu
To say	Asel
Something	Inch vor ban / mi ban
To go	Gnal
Ready	Patrast
Soon	Shut / Shutov
To work	Ashkhatel [aʃ xatél]
Who	Ov
Important	Karevor

I like to be at home with my parents
Yes sirum em linel tany tsnoghneris het
I want to know why I must say something important
Yes uzum em imanal, inchu yes petq e asem karevor ban
(karevor - important, ban - something)
I am there with him
Yes ayntegh em nra het
I am busy, but I need to be ready soon
Yes zbaghvats em, bayc petq e linem patrast shutov
I like to work
Yes sirum em ashkhatel
Who is there?
Ov e ayntegh?
I want to know if they are here, because I want to go outside
Yes uzum em imanal ardyoq nranq aystegh em, vorovhetev uzum em gnal durs
There are seven dolls
Kan yot tiknikner

I love	Yes sirum em
How much	Vorqan / (about price) Inch azhe
To take	Vertsnel
With me	Indz het
Instead	Pokharen
Only	Miayn
When	Yerb
I can / Can I	Yes karogh em / Yes karogh em?
Or	Kam
Were	Ein
Without me	Arants indz
Fast	Arag
Slow	Dandagh
Cold	Sary [sarə]
Inside	Mej / Nersum
To eat	Utel
Hot	Taq
To Drive	Varel

How much money do I need to take?
Inchqan pogh yes petq e vercnem?
Only when you can
Miayn yerb karoghanas/karoghanaq (formal, plural)
They were without me yesterday
Nranq arants indz ein yerek
I need to drive the car very fast or very slowly
Yes petq e varem meqenan shat arag kam shat tandagh
It is cold in the library
Gradaranum tsurt e
(gradaranum - in the library, tsurt e - it is cold)
Yes, I like to eat this hot
Ayo, yes uzum em utel sa taq

The Program

World	Ashkharhov
To answer	Pataskhanel
To fly	Trchel
Yours	Qo, qonn/Dzer (formal, plural)
To travel	Chanaparhordel
To learn	Sovorel
Children	Yerekhaner
To swim	Loghal
To practice	Parapel
To play	Khaghal
To leave	Gnal / Meknel (far)
Many/much/a lot	Shat
I go to	Yes gnum em
First	Araji
Time / Times	Angam

I need to answer many questions
Yes petq e pataskhanem shat hartseri
I want to fly today
Yes uzum em trchel aysor
I need to learn to swim
Yes petq e sovorem loghal
I want to leave this here for you, when I go to travel the world
Yes uzum em toghnel sa aystegh qez hamar, yerb yes meknem chanaparhelu ashkharhov
Since the first time
Araji angamits
The children are yours
Yerekhanery [erexanerə] qonn en
I need the books
Indz petq en grqery

*In Armenian, both *qo* and *qonn* are used to signify "yours," however, *qonn* is used to define particular cases, i.e. particular children.
*With the knowledge you've gained so far, now try to create your own sentences!

Nobody	Vochvoq
Against	Dem
Us / we	Menq
To visit	Aytselel
Mom / Mother	Mama / Mayr
To give	Tal
Which	Vor
To meet	Handipel
Someone	Meky/inch vor meki
Just	Miayn
To walk	Qaylel
Around	Shurj
Family	Yntaniq [əntanik]
Than	Qan
Nothing	Vochinch
Week	Shabat

Something is better than nothing
Inch vor ban aveli lav e qan vochinch
I am against him
Yes dem em nran
We go each week to visit my family
Menq gnum enq amen shabat aytselelu im yntaniqy [əntaníkə]
I need to give you something
Yes petq e tam qez mi ban
Do you want to meet someone?
Du uzum es tesnel inch vor meki?
(formal, plural) Duq uzum eq tesnel inch vor meki?
I am here also on Wednesdays
Yes aystegh em nuynpes choreqshabti orery
You do this everyday?
Du anum es sa amen or?
You need to walk around the house
Du petq e qayles tan shurjy

*If you notice the sentences above, to signify "something" both i*nch vor ban* and *mi ban* are used. The sentence *yes petq e tam qez mi ban*, *mi ban* is used instead of *inch vor ban*. In this case, the word "something" is translated as one thing /*mi ban*. Because you know exactly what it is you need to give, you just don't want to name it. If you don't know what you are going to give, and you are thinking about what to give, in that case it would be OK to say *inch vor ban*.

*Concerning "someone," both *meki* or *inch vor meki* can be used. It depends on the case, in a similar way to "something." If you know who it is, but you don't name them for some reason, then it will be *meki*, but if you are not sure about who the person is, then it will be *inch vor meki*.

Orery literally means "days" in Armenian. "On Wednesday" will be said as *choreqshabti orery* meaning "Wednesday days."

The Program

I have	Yes unem
Don't	Mi
Friend	Ynker [ənkér]
To borrow	vertsnel / partqov vertsnel
To look like	Tesq unenal / nmanvel
Grandfather	Papik / pap
To want	Uzel / Tsankanal
To stay	Mnal
To continue	Sharunakel
Way	Chanaparh
That's why	Aha te inchu
To show	Tsuyts tal
To prepare	Patrastel
I am not going	Yes chem gnum
How	Inchpes / (informal)Vonts

Do you want to look like Arnold?
Du uzum es nmanvel Arnoldin?
I want to borrow this book for my grandfather
Yes uzum em vertsnel ays girqy papikis hamar
I want to drive and to continue on this way to my house
Yes uzum em varel yev gnal ays chanaparhov depi im tuny
I have a friend, that's why I want to stay with him in Yerevan
Yes unem ynker, aha te inchu uzum em mnal nra het Yerevan
I don't want to see anyone here
Yes chem uzum tesnel voch voqi aystegh
I need to show you how to prepare breakfast
Yes petq e tsuyts tam qez inchpes patrastel nakhachash
Why don't you have the book?
Inchu du chunes girqy?
I don't need the car today
Indz petq chi meqenan aysor

Depi means "towards."
*In Armenian, ch is used for the purpose of negation, and usually merges with the verb. "Why don't you have the book?" *Inchu du chunes* (*unes* means "you have," *ch* means "don't") *girqy*?

To remember	Hishel
Armenian	Hayeren
Number	Hamar / tiv
Hour	Zham
Dark / darkness	Mut / mtutyun
About	Masin
Grandmother	Tatik / tat
Five	Hing
Minute / Minutes	Rope [ropé]
More	Shat / aveli shat
To think	Mtatsel
To do	Anel
To come	Gal
To hear	Lsel
Last	Verjin
To speak	Khosel

I need to remember this number
Yes petq e hishem ays hamary
This is the last hour
Sa verjin zhamn e
I want to hear my grandmother speak English today
Yes uzum em lsel tatikis angleren khosely aysor
I need to think more about this, and what to do
Yes petq e aveli shat mtatsem sra masin, yev te inch anel
From here to there it's five minutes
Aysteghits ayntegh hing rope e

The Program

To leave	Gnal
Again	Norits / krkin
Armenia	Hayastan
To bring	Berel
To try	Pordzel
To rent	Vardzel
Without her	Arants nra
We are	Menq enq
To turn off	Anjatel
To ask	Hartsnel
To stop	Kangnetsnel
Permission	Tuyltvutyun

He needs to rent a house at the beach
Na petq e vardzi mi tun tsovapin
Tonight I need to turn off the lights early
Ays gisher yes petq e shut anjatem luysery [luisérə]
(shut - early, anjatem - turn off, luysery - the lights)
We want to stop here
Menq uzum enq kang arnel aystegh
We are from Vanadzoric
Menq Vanadzoric enq
The same building
Nuyn shenqy
I want to ask for permission to leave
Yes uzum em tuyltvutyun khndrel gnalu
Can I leave?
Karogh em gnal?

*Ays gisher – "this night," "tonight".
*Aysor yerekoyan – "tonight," "this evening"
*In Armenian to signify "stop" we use *kangnetsne*, however *kang arnel* and *dadarel* can be used as well.

To open	Batsel
To buy	Gnel
To pay	Vcharel
Last	Verjin
Without	Arants
Sister	Quyr
To hope	Husal / huys unenal
To live	Aprel
Nice to meet you	Hacheli e tsanotanal
Name	Anun
Last name	Azganun
To return	Vernut'sya
Future	Apaga
Door	Dur
Our	Mer
On	Vra

I need to open the door for my sister
Yes petq e dury batsem qrojs hamar
I need to buy something
Yes petq e mi ban arnem
I want to get to know your sisters
Yes uzum em tsanotanal quyrerid het
Nice to meet you, what is your name and your last name?
Hacheli e tsanotanal, inch e dzer anuny u azganuny?
To hope for the better in the future
Husal vor apagayum lav klini
Why are you sad right now?
Inchu es tkhur hima?
Our house is on the hill
Mer tuny blri vra e

*If you noticed in the sentences above, to signify "sister" both *quyr* and *qroj* are used. *Quyr* is the straight form of sister; "for my sister" is a declined form. In Armenian, there are different declensions of nouns. So "for my sister" will be *qrojs hamar* (*qrojs* – the declined form of "my sister," and *hamar* – "for") the *s* at the end of *qrojs* means that it is "my sister." If it were for "her sister," it would be – *nra qroj hamar*.
*"To hope" / *huys unenal* literally means "to have hope" (*huys* - "hope", *unenal* - "to have").
*This *isn't* a phrase book! The purpose of this book is *solely* to provide you with the tools to create *your own* sentences!

The Program

To happen	Patahel
To order	Patvirel
To drink	Khmel
Excuse me	Knereq/neroghutyun
Child	Yerekha
Woman	Kin
To begin / To start	Sqsel
To finish	Verjatsnel
To help	Ognel
To smoke	Tskhel
To love	Sirel
To talk / To Speak	Khosel

This must happen today
Sa petq e teghi unena aysor
Excuse me, my child is here as well
Knereq, im yerekhan el e aystegh
I love you
Yes sirum em qez
I see you
Yes tesnum em qez
I need you
Du indz petq es
(Du - you, indz - to me, petq es - are necessary) /
Yes qo kariqn unem
(yes - I, qo - your, kariq - need, unem - have)
I want to help
Yes uzum em ognel
I don't want to smoke again
Yes chem uzum tskhel krkin
I want to learn to speak Armenian
Yes uzum em sovorel khosel hayeren

To read	Kardal
To write	Grel
To teach	Sovoretsnel / dasavandel
To close	Pakel
To turn on	Miatsnel
To prefer	Nakhyntrel [naxəntrél]
To put	Dnel
Less	Aveli qich
Sun	Arev
Month	Amis
I Talk	Yes khosum em
Exact	Chshgrit
To choose	Yntrel [əntrél]
In order to	Vorpiszi

I need this book, in order to learn how to read and write in Armenian
Indz petq e ays girqy, vorpiszi sovorel kardal yev grel Hayeren
I want to teach in Armenia
Yes uzum em dasavandel Hayastanum
I want to close the door of the house and not to turn on the light
Yes uzum em pakel tan dury yev chmiatsnel luysy
I prefer to put the gift here
Yes nakhyntrum em dnel nvery aystegh
I want to pay less than you for the dinner
Yes uzum em vcharel aveli qich qan du chashi hamar
I speak with the boy and the girl in Armenian
Yes khosum em tghayi yev aghjka het hayeren
I see the sun today
Yes tesnum em arev aysor
Is it possible to know the exact day?
Hnaravor e imanal chshgrit ory?

The Program

To exchange	Pokhel
To call	Zangaharel / (informal) zangel
Brother	Yeghbayr
Dad	Papa / hayrik
To sit	Nstel
Together	Miasin
To change	Pokhel
Of course	Iharke
Welcome	Bari galust
During	Yntatsqum [əntatskum]
Years	Tariner
Sky	Yerkinq
Up	Verev
Down	Nerqev
Sorry	Kneres / (formal, plural) knereq
To follow	Hetevel
Her	Na
Big	Mets
New	Nor
Never	Yerbeq

I don't want to exchange this money at the bank
Yes chem uzum pokhanakel ays poghy bankum
Today I want to call my brother and my dad
Aysor yes uzum em zangel yeghbors u hors
Of course I can come to the theater, and I want to sit together with you and with your sister
Iharke yes uzum em gal tatron, yev uzum em nstel miasin qo yev qrojd het
I need to see your new house
Yes petq e tesnem qo nor tuny
I can see the sky from the window
Yes karogh em tesnel yerkinqy patuhanits

To allow	Tuyl tal / tuylatrel
To believe	Havatal
Morning	Aravot
Except	Batsi
To promise	Khostanal
Good night	Bari gisher
To recognize	Chanachel
People	Mardik
To move	Sharzhvel
To move (to a place)	Teghapokhvel
Far	Heru
Different	Other
Man	Tghamard
To enter	Mtnel
To receive	Stanal
Tonight	Aysor yerekoyan
Through	Mijov
Him / his	Nra

I believe everything except for this
Yes havatum em amen inchin baci sranits
They need to recognize the Armenian people quickly
Nranq petq e chanachen hay mardkants arag
I need to move your cat to another chair
Yes petq e teghapokhem qo katvin urish atorin
I see the sun in the morning from the kitchen
Yes tesnum em arevy aravotyan khohanotsits
I want his car
Yes uzum em nra meqenan

*With the knowledge you've gained so far, now try to create your own sentences!

To wish	Uzel / tsankanal
Bad	Vat
To Get	Stanal / charel
To forget	Moranal
Everybody / Everyone	Bolory
Although	Chnayats
To feel	Zgal
Great	Mets
Next	Hajord, myus
To like	Sirel / havanel / dur gal
In front	Arjevum
Person	Andz / mard
Behind	Hetevum
Well	Lav
Goodbye	Tsy [tsə] tesutyun/haj oghutyun
Restaurant	Restoran
Bathroom	Baghniq / zugaran (toilet)

I don't want to wish anything bad
Chem uzum tsankanal voch mi vat ban
I must forget everybody from my past
Yes petq e moranam bolorin im antsyalits
I am close to the person behind you
Yes aveli mot em mardun, vor qo hetevum e
I say goodbye to my friends
Yes hrazhesht em talis ynkerneris
In which part of the restaurant is the bathroom?
Restorani vor masum e zugarany?
I want a car before the next year
Yes uzum em meqena minchev hajord tari
I like the house, however it is very small
Yes havanum em tuny, bayts ayn shat poqr e

To remove	Veratsnel
Please	Khndrem
Beautiful	Geghetsik / sirun
To lift	Bardzratsnel
Include / Including	Neraryal
Belong	Patkanel
To hold	Pahel
To check	Stugel
Small	Poqr
Real	Iskakan / irakan
Week	Shabat
Size	Chap
Even though	Nuynisk ete
Doesn't	Chi
So	Ayspisov
Price	Gin

She wants to remove this door
Na uzum e veratsnel dury
This doesn't belong here
Aystegh sra teghy chi
(Aystegh - here, sra - for this, teghy - the place, chi - not)
I need to check again
Yes petq e stugem krkin
This week the weather was very beautiful
Ays shabat yeghanaky shat geghetsik er
I need to know which is the real diamond
Yes petq e imanam vorn e iskakan adamandy
We need to check the size of the house
Menq petq e stugenq tan chapy
I can pay this although the price is expensive
Yes karogh em vcharel sa, chnayats giny tank e
Is everything included in this price?
Ameninch nerarvats e ays gni mej?

BUILDING BRIDGES

In Building Bridges, we take six conjugated verbs that have been selected after studies I have conducted for several months in order to determine which verbs are most commonly conjugated, and which are then automatically followed by an infinitive verb. For example, once you know how to say, "I need," "I want," "I can," and "I like," you will be able to connect words and say almost anything you want more correctly and understandably. The following three pages contain these six conjugated verbs in first, second, third, fourth, and fifth person, as well as some sample sentences. Please master the entire program up until *here* prior to venturing onto this section.

I want	Yes uzum em
I need	Indz petq e
I can	Yes karogh em
I like	Indz dur e galis/yes sirum em
I go	Yes gnum em
I have to/ I must	Yes petq e
To have	Yes unem

I want to go to my apartment
Yes uzum em gnal im bnakaran
I can go with you to the bus station
Yes karogh em gnal qez het avtobusi kayan
I need to walk to the museum
Yes petq e qaylem depi tangaran
I like the train
Indz dur e galis gnatsqy
I want to teach a class
Yes uzum em das tal
I have to speak to my teacher
Yes petq e xosem usutschis/dasatuis het

Please master pages #16-#38, prior to attempting the following two pages!!

You want / do you want? - Du uzum es / Du uzum es?
He wants / does he want? - Na uzum e / Na uzum e?
She wants / does she want? - Na uzum e / Na uzum e?
We want / do we want? - Menq uzum enq / Menq uzum enq?
They want / do they want? - Nranq uzum en / Nranq uzum en?
You (plural/ formal sing) want - Duq uzum eq / Duq uzum eq?

You need / do you need? - Qez petq e / Qez petq e?
He needs / does he need? - Nran petq e / Nran petq e?
She needs / does she need? - Nran petq e / Nran petq e?
We Need / do we need? - Mez petq e / Mez petq e?
They need / do they need? - Nrants petq e / Nrants petq e?
You (plural/ formal sing) need - Dzez petq e / Dzez petq e?

You can / can you? - Du karogh es / Du karogh es ?
He can / can he? - Na karogh e / Na karogh e?
She can / can she? - Na karogh e / Na karogh e?
We can / can we? - Menq karogh enq / Menq karogh enq?
They can / can they? - Nranq karogh en / Nranq karogh en?
You (plural/ formal sing) can - Duq karogh eq / Duq karogh eq?

You like / do you like? - Qez dur e galis / Qez dur e galis?
He likes / does he like? - Nran dur e galis / Nran dur e galis?
She like / does she like? - Nran dur e galis / Nran dur e galis?
We like / do we like? - Mez dur e galis / Mez dur e galis?
They like / do they like? - Nrants dur e galis / Nrants dur e galis?
You (plural/ formal sing) like -Dzez dur e galis / Dzez dur e galis?

You go / do you go? - Du gnum es / Du gnum es?
He goes / does he go? - Na gnum e / Na gnum e?
She goes / does she go? - Na gnum e / Na gnum e?
We go / do we go? - Menq gnum enq / Menq gnum enq?
They go / do they go? - Nranq gnum en / Nranq gnum en?
You (plural/ formal sing) go - Duq gnum eq / Duq gnum eq?

You must / do you have to - Du petq e / Du petq e?
He must / does he have to - Na petq e / Na petq e?
She must / does she have to - Na petq e / Na petq e?
We have / do we have to - Menq petq e / Menq petq e?
They must / do they have to - Nranq petq e / Nranq petq e?
You (plural/ formal sing) must - Duq petq e / Duq petq e?

You have - Du unes
He has - Na uni
She has - Na uni
We have - Menq unenq
They have - Nranq unen
You (plural) have - Duq uneq

Please master pages #16-#39, prior to attempting the following page!!

Do you want to go?
Uzum es gnal?
(plural/ formal sing) Uzum eq gnal?
Does he want to fly?
Na uzum e trnel?
We want to swim
Menq uzum enq loghal
Do they want to run?
Nranq uzum en vazel?
Do you need to clean?
Du petq e maqres?
She needs to sing a song
Na petq e yergi mi yerg
We need to travel
Menq petq e meknenq (leave) / chanapahordenq (travel)
They don't need to fight
Nranq chpetq e krven
You (plural) need to see the film
Duq petq e tesneq filmy
Can you hear me?
Du indz lsum es?
He can dance very well
Na karoghanum e parel shat lav
We can go out tonight
Menq karogh enq durs gal aysor yerekoyan *(durs gal - go out, aysor - today, yerekoyan - evening)*
They can break the wood
Nranq karogh en kotrel payty [paytə]
Do you like to eat here?
Du uzum es utel aystegh?

He likes to spend time here
Na sirum e zhamanak ants katsnel aystegh
We like to fix the house
Mez dur e galis noroqel tuny
They like to cook
Nranq sirum en patrastel
You (plural) like my house
Dzez dur e galis im tuny
Do you go to school today?
Du gnum es dprots aysor?
He goes fishing
Na gnum e dzknorsutyan
We are going to relax
Menq patrastvum enq hangstanal
They go to watch a film
Nranq gnum en ditelu mi film
Do you have money?
Du unes pogh/dram?
She must look outside
Na petq e nayi durs
We have to sign here
Menq petq e storagrenq aystegh
They have to send the letter
Nranq petq e ugharken namaky
You (plural) have to order
Duq petq e patvireq

Days of the Week

Sunday	Kiraki
Monday	Yerkushabti
Tuesday	Yereqshabti
Wednesday	Choreqshabti
Thursday	Hingshabti
Friday	Urbat
Saturday	Shabat

Seasons

Spring	Garun
Summer	Amar
Autumn	Ashun
Winter	Dzmer

Cardinal Directions

North	Hyusis
South	Harav
East	Arevelq
West	Arevmutq

Colors

Black	Sev
White	Spitak
Gray	Mokhraguyn / Gorsh
Red	Karmir
Blue	Kapuyt
Yellow	Deghin
Green	Kanach
Orange	Narnjaguyn
Purple	Manushakaguyn
Brown	Shaganakaguyn *or* Darchnaguyn

Numbers

One	Mek
Two	Yerku
Three	Yereq
Four	Chors
Five	Hing
Six	Vets
Seven	Yot
Eight	Ut
Nine	Inny [innə]
Ten	Tas

CONGRATULATIONS, NOW YOU ARE ON YOUR OWN!

If you merely absorb the required three hundred and fifty words in this book, you will then have acquired the basis to become conversational in **Armenian**! After memorizing these three hundred and fifty words, this conversational foundational basis that you have just gained will trigger your ability to make improvements in conversational fluency at an amazing speed! However, in order to engage in quick and easy conversational communication, you need a special type of basics, and this book will provide you with just that.

Unlike the foreign language learning systems presently used in schools and universities, along with books and programs that are available on the market today, that focus on *everything* but being conversational, *this* method's sole focus is on becoming conversational in **Armenian** as well as any other language. Once you have successfully mastered the required words in this book, there are two techniques that if combined with these essential words, can further enhance your skills and will result in you improving your proficiency tenfold. *However*, these two techniques will only succeed *if* you have completely and successfully absorbed the three hundred and fifty words. *After* you establish the basis for fluent communications by memorizing these words, you can enhance your conversational abilities even more if you use the following two techniques.

The first step is to attend a **Armenian** language class that will enable you to sharpen your grammar. You will gain additional vocabulary and learn past and present tenses, and if you apply these skills that you learn in the class, together with the three hundred and fifty words that you have previously memorized, you will be improving your conversational skills tenfold. You will notice that, conversationally, you will succeed at a much higher rate than any of your classmates. A simple second technique is to choose Armenian subtitles while watching a movie. If you have successfully mastered and grasped these three hundred and fifty words, then the combination of the two—those words along with the subtitles—will aid you considerably in putting all the grammar into perspective, and again, conversationally, you will improve tenfold.

Once you have established a basis of quick and easy conversation in Armenian with those words that you just attained, every additional word or grammar rule you pick up from there on will be gravy. And these additional words or grammar rules can be combined with the three hundred and fifty words, enriching your conversational abilities even more. Basically, after the research and studies I've conducted with my method over the years, I came to the conclusion that in order to become conversational, you first must learn the words and then learn the grammar.

The Armenian language is compatible with the mirror translation technique. Likewise, with this language, you can use this mirror translation technique in order to become conversational, enabling you to communicate even more effortlessly. Mirror translation is the method of translating a phrase or sentence, word for word from English to Armenian, by using these imperative words that you have acquired through this program (such as the sentences I used in this book. Latin languages, Middle Eastern languages, and Slavic languages, along with a few others, are also compatible with the mirror translation technique. Though you won't be speaking perfectly proper and precise Armenian, you will still be fully understood and, conversation-wise, be able to get by just fine.

CONCLUSION

Congratulations! You have completed all the tools needed to master the **Armenian** language, and I hope that this has been a valuable learning experience. Now you have sufficient communication skills to be confident enough to embark on a visit to Armenia, impress your friends, and boost your resume so good luck.

This program is available in other languages as well, and it is my fervent hope that my language learning programs will be used for good, enabling people from all corners of the globe and from all cultures and religions to be able to communicate harmoniously. After memorizing the required three hundred and fifty words, please perform a daily five-minute exercise by creating sentences in your head using these words. This simple exercise will help you grasp conversational communications even more effectively. Also, once you memorize the vocabulary on each page, follow it by using a notecard to cover the words you have just memorized and test yourself and follow that by going back and using this same notecard technique on the pages you studied during the previous days. This repetition technique will assist you in mastering these words in order to provide you with the tools to create your own sentences.

Every day, use this notecard technique on the words that you have just studied.

Everything in life has a catch. The catch here is just consistency. If you just open the book, and after the first few pages of studying the program, you put it down, then you will not gain anything. However, if you consistently dedicate a half hour daily to studying, as well as reviewing what you have learned from previous days, then you will quickly realize why this method is the most effective technique ever created to become conversational in a foreign language. My technique works! For anyone who doubts this technique, all I can say is that it has worked for me and hundreds of others.

Note from the Author

Thank you for your interest in my work. I encourage you to share your overall experience of this book by posting a review. Your review can make a difference! Please feel free to describe how you benefited from my method or provide creative feedback on how I can improve this program. I am constantly seeking ways to enhance the quality of this product, based on personal testimonials and suggestions from individuals like you.
Thanks and best of luck,
Yatir Nitzany

www.ingramcontent.com/pod-product-compliance
Lightning Source LLC
Chambersburg PA
CBHW052107110526
44591CB00013B/2381